THE
GATES

———

Access to the Throne of God

———

SHALAYNA JANELLE

THE

GATES

———

Access to the Throne of God

———

SHALAYNA JANELLE

The Gates by Shalayna Janelle

Published by SJI Publishing House

Los Angeles, CA

WWW.ShalaynaJanelle.com

For Worldwide Distribution, Printed in the United States of America.
(Unless otherwise noted on the last page of this book)

All scriptures and scripture quotations are from the King James
Version of the Bible (Public Domain).

Unless otherwise noted all poems and prayers are copyright of
Shalayna Janelle.

Author Photo credit: Nick Krakovski

Library of Congress Control Number: 2016908944

ISBN: 978-0-692-76338-4

Dedication

To the Father, Son, and the Holy Ghost.
For teaching me, leading me and guiding me to all truth.

You taught me how to truly worship. It is most definitely a
blessing to worship you with my life!

Contents

First Things First

If you have just stumbled upon this book and may not know Jesus and have not accepted Him as your personal Lord and Savior, I just want to let you know that you are loved! Jesus loves YOU so much! He died for you; He put Himself on the line just for you to be forgiven of your sins. The Bible says:

"For God so loved the world that He gave his only begotten son, that whosoever believes in him shall not perish but have everlasting life"
(John 3:16).

"Surely he hath borne our griefs, and carried our sorrows: yet we did esteem him stricken, smitten of God, and afflicted. But he was wounded for our transgressions. He was bruised for our iniquities: the chastisement of our peace was upon him; and with his stripes we are healed"
(Isaiah 53:4,5).

"God commendeth his love toward us, in that, while we were yet sinners, Christ died for us"
(Romans 5:8).

I would also like to give you an opportunity to accept Jesus Christ as your personal **Lord** and Savior. Ask Him into your heart. You may use the prayer on the following page:

"Dear Precious Lord,
Thank you for this chance at salvation that you have given me because you love me. I acknowledge that I am a sinner and I have done things that have displeased you and broke your heart. In sincerity I repent and ask that you forgive me for my sins and give me a clean and righteous heart. I believe your scriptures that say Jesus Christ came to earth to die for the sins of the world. This includes me.
With no doubt, I know and believe that Jesus Christ your only begotten son lived for my sake, suffered for my sake, died for my sake and has risen from the grave for my sake, and it is through my belief in Him that I can be saved and have eternal life.
Because I believe, I make room for you Jesus in my life and heart today, from here on out. I lay down every idol, please take your place as the only Master, Lord and Savior of my life.
I thank you Jesus for forgiving my sins, saving me and giving me new life in you. I commit to walking with you forever.
In Jesus' name. Amen."
-Shalayna Janelle

Welcome to the Family!

This prayer is a confession of your new found faith in Jesus Christ. If you've truly repented and believe this in your heart you are now born again! Not by simply reciting a prayer but it is by your sincere repentance and belief in Christ, His work on the cross and His resurrection that makes you born again.

For more information on salvation and the next steps to take as a new believer feel free to visit the link below!

http://shalaynajanelle.com/realtalkyo-blog/blog/want-to-be-saved-how-can-i-be-saved-i-ve-accepted-jesus-whats-next

Introduction

Worship? Really! A book on worship? Why? Worship is a very complex subject. God speaks about it in the Bible directly and indirectly. In my experiences with God, I came to know Him more through worship. I also came to understand that worship wasn't all that the mainstream tells us it is. There are more dynamics to worship than the average Christian may know of. That's why I wrote this book!

My goal in everything that I do is to lead people to Jesus Christ. Or, to lead those who are already following Him closer to Him. I aspire to see a generation fully engulfed in God, relating to Him in a variety of ways because they have a deep passionate love for Him. It's not about imitation. It's not imitating this or that preacher, this brother or sister in Christ, pastors—not imitating me. It's about developing your own relationship—a passionate relationship with the Lord where you allow Him to show you who you are according to His Word. Knowing who God truly is, is the key to dealing with EVERYTHING we will face in our entire walk with Him. We can't afford to miss out on truly knowing our precious God.

I like to think of myself as a builder. A Kingdom Builder! I want to help people build and build and continue to build their relationship with God. To get individuals to leave the clichés and step into the Spirit. You can't ever have too much of Jesus— right?

Truth is, I never really had anyone who would take the time to encourage me to this degree. What I want people to take from my books is that Jesus is the "end all, be all." Yup! I said it! Jesus deserves the glory, honor, and praise in and through our lives. Not me or any other person. I'm just the vessel as we all are when being used by God!

Having said that, if you want to grow in God and your heart's desire is to truly honor and worship Him with purpose and devotion, then you have chosen the perfect book to start your journey.

Chapter 1
The Misconception

What is worship? One of the greatest misconceptions about worship is that it's just one of many parts of a church service. Another mistaken belief is that it's an overwhelming sense that comes over you when music is played! If we were to ask many of our peers, friends, churchgoers and others what worship is, chances are, they will more than likely associate it with a song and nothing else. Yes, you can worship God with songs and while the music is playing. But the songs and music are not what causes one to worship. Music is not where it starts.

So what is worship? According to *Oxford Dictionaries.com,* the definition of worship is "The feeling or expression of reverence and adoration for a deity." First of all, worship starts by acknowledging that there is a God (Jesus) who is higher than anything. Then, you must allow that to resonate in your heart. Worship is more than just a song. A song in itself does not have the ability to make you worship if your heart isn't already in worship to God. If you don't reverence God, a melody does not make you reverence Him. Only the Holy Spirit can draw someone in that manner (John 6:44).

Worship from the heart is reflected in the lives we live. "But the hour cometh, and now is, when the true worshippers shall worship the Father in spirit and in truth: for the Father seeketh such to worship him." John 4:23 "God is a spirit: and they that worship him must worship him in spirit and truth" (John 4:24).

~Truth~

Luke 2:36-38 briefly references a woman named Anna. Anna was a prophetess whom God used to evangelize to people about the birth of Christ. When she saw Jesus, she recognized immediately that He was the Savior of the world.

Now, the interesting part of Anna's story is that she was an older woman whose husband had died. Instead of remarrying, she decided to stay in the temple fasting, praying and worshiping God day and night. I absolutely LOVE the eagerness and willingness of fully dedicating our entire lives to the service of God.

Day and night—night and day worshiping the Lord! What would it look like to worship the Lord day and night? Interesting huh? That's what we were created to do!

I enjoy likening it to a king who has a kingdom (In fact, JESUS IS A KING who has a kingdom, so this analogy works PERFECTLY). In a king's kingdom, there are gates that separate the inner courts from the outer courts. Gates keep people from tapping into something they have no credentials to get to. One would have to be granted permission to get past those gates and into the inner courts. Oh, did I mention there are also gatekeepers guarding the gates? Those are the people who let or take people into the inner courts. (But that's another topic for another book).

The king resides inside the gates, which is where you want to be—in the presence of the king! This is where your petition can be heard. This is where you have the king's full attention!

God is in the temple—in the inner courts! We must get to the inner courts but we can only do so if we get past the gates. I want to help you get through the gates!

I wrote this book for those who may not be too familiar

with true worship, those who don't understand worship, and lastly for those who want to grow in God. Some even say: "Oh it's the Bible. I can't do what those people in the Bible did." Well, why not? Many of us are! The prophetess Anna did it, and she was human just like you and me!

Jesus said that true worshipers would come and worship Him in spirit and in truth. If it wasn't possible, He wouldn't have advocated it.

Now, I believe in you because Jesus believed in me! I don't doubt that you can live a life worshiping God day and night. It's in your DNA. DNA is beneath the flesh. So it takes getting out of the flesh to do this. If it wasn't, God wouldn't have let this book touch your hands. I'm convinced that you don't want to stay outside the gates, you want to be inside with the king day and night, having front row seats and personal experiences with the king! The KING of KINGS!

Now, let's thank God for the divine opportunity, for where He is taking you. For the walls that He's tearing down right now in the spirit. The armor He's putting on you. The utensils He's sharpening and for the grace He has bestowed upon you.

Now let's "Enter into his **Gates** with thanksgiving, and into his **Courts** with praise: be thankful unto him, and bless his name" (Psalm 100:4).

Chapter 2
Lifestyle of Worship

There used to be a magazine called *Lifestyle Magazine*. Who knows—maybe it's still around. I don't really keep up with that stuff. However, when you see this magazine, immediately, you know what it is about. Not based on its title alone but the cover of the magazine will reflect what's inside of it; photos and topics related to lifestyles will be highlighted on the front. Automatically, you know "Ok, that's *Lifestyle Magazine*." It's quite similar to how you can look at the cover of a tabloid and know it's a tabloid with its sensational stories and gossip. *Home & Furniture* magazines will reflect what's inside of them by projecting furniture on their covers. Nothing reflected on the cover of those magazines is by accident. The magazine's cover is deliberately designed to show on the outside what the inside is ALL about.

Similarly, who we are, what we are and what we do on the outside are clearly reflections of what is on the inside and can be seen by our behaviors, attitudes, and the way we live. So, by now, you probably see that there's more to worship than meets the stereotype. Worship at its core is a lifestyle. Lifestyle speaks of the way a person or group lives—their life, conduct, behavior, customs, habits and ways. Living a lifestyle of worship starts with submission!

Often times, many people get saved and say: "My life is not my own." But, do you really believe it? Is your lifestyle really reflecting it? When you wake up each day who are you really living for? When you go to bed at night can you say that your day was lived for God—or for you? Can you say that you truly did your best to live out what God has told you to do for that day? The **goal** is for the answers to those questions to always be yes! The reality is, however, that many Christians aren't dedicated enough for the answers to those questions to be "yes." Wow! Can you imagine walking out the door and based on how you decide to live and handle situations, your lifestyle reflected everything except what God intended you to do? That's Scary!

You see, the difference between a moment of worship and a lifestyle of worship is just a decision. There came a point in my life when I had to make a decision to worship God with my life—it wasn't presented to me as if it was a decision, but it was one. Often times, we don't realize we're constantly making decisions. But, the reality is that everything we do is based on the decisions we make. I love to quote this scripture:

> *And if it seem evil unto you to serve the LORD, choose you this day whom ye will serve; whether the gods which your fathers served that were on the other side of the flood, or the gods of the Amorites, in whose land ye dwell:* **but** *as for* **me** *and* **my house,** *we will serve the LORD.*
> *Joshua 24:15*

As stated previously, a lifestyle of worship starts with submission! A perfect example of submission is shown in Matt 26:39:

"And he went a little farther, and fell on his face, and prayed, saying, O my Father, if it be possible, let this cup pass from me: **nevertheless not as I will, but as thou wilt.** *"* Jesus was and still is our ultimate example of how to live. In this particular verse, He was about to be betrayed and led to the

cross. He could have used His "glorious rising from the dead power" to change and prevent this whole situation from happening. That wasn't an option for Him because He understood the importance of His submission. He knew that the way He lived would affect the lives of others. He understood the responsibility that He carried! His heart made a conscious decision to submit totally to the Father so that His complete purpose may be fulfilled.

This is an awesome time to just reflect and ask:

"What does my life look like to you Lord?"

"Do you see me as a submitted vessel?"

"Am I as close to you God as I could be or should be?"

"Lord, have I been with you so much that people can see my cover showing that you are on the inside of me?"

"God, does my life worship you?"

"Have I dedicated my whole life as worship to you?" (Rom 12:1)

"Or have I never really seen worship as even a lifestyle?"

Those are some questions to ask God and yourself. Truly, take the time to see where you stand—not so you can see if you're bad or good but because you have to know where you are in order to see what your next step will be. This is actually a method to apply in your walk with God for a lifetime. It's based on 2 Cor 13:5: *"Examine yourselves, whether ye be in the faith; prove your own selves. Know ye not your own selves, how that Jesus Christ is in you, except ye be reprobates?"* It's always useful to examine ourselves to see where we stand.

Just like that *Lifestyle Magazine* we want to really have the experience of what's on the cover actually truly being on the inside of us. We want people to be able to tell exactly who we live for by the way we live our lives, how we act, what we say, and what we participate in. Are you striving for that? Are you running toward that? Are you willing to do it?

"Know ye not that they which run in a race all, but one receiveth

the prize? And every man that striveth for the mastery is **temperate** *in* **all things.** *Now they do it to obtain a corruptible crown; but we an incorruptible. I therefore so run, not as uncertainly; so fight I, not as one that beateth the air: but I keep under my body, and bring it into subjection: lest that by any means, when I have preached to others, I myself should be a castaway."*
1 Cor 9: 24 - 27

In the previous scripture, the word "temperate" is used. **Temperate** means showing moderation or self-restraint. In other words, it means to change some things up for better in order to function in this race properly—to be able to discipline ourselves. In fact, it takes **discip**line in order to be a **discip**le.

In these next chapters, we will discuss a little deeper, the ways to fully live our lives in full service and worship to God. But first, I want to leave you with some characteristics of a disciple:

- Follower of a teacher (Matt 20:17) (Luke 18:31).
- Servant (Matt 10:24) (Matt 20:26-28).
- Focused on God and the kingdom (Heb 5:7-9).
- Disciplined (core of being a disciple) (1 Cor 9:24-27).

What are we patterning our lives after? Can people tell our influences by spending a day with us? Are we disciplined in our speech? Disciplined in the Word? When I made the decision to let God have my whole life, my goal was to make sure that I got to know Him so well that my life would begin to take on His nature. It's often said, "You are who you hang around the most." Or "Show me the 5 people you hang around the most, and I can tell you who you are." What if Jesus became one of the 5? Can you imagine the effect your life would have on people? Even on complete strangers. I was then and still am determined to do what it takes to get to where God needs me to be in any particular season.

After all, I did commit to a "lifestyle of worship."

Lifestyle does mean life and everything pertaining to it. Nothing was off limits for God to touch. This may seem uncomfortable to some, but I am beyond blessed by the one decision to surrender my life to God! I know you will be too!

Lastly, I'd like to add that a lifestyle of worship to Jesus can only be done with the help of the Holy Spirit. The Holy Spirit is our **helper, keeper, comforter** (John 14:16, 26), **teacher** (John 14:26) and **spirit of truth** (John 14:17, 16:13). It is by Him that we are sustained and even set apart.

I can't assume that everyone knows about the Holy Spirit. So, I would rather explain than to leave you in wonder if you don't know. The Holy Spirit is one of the free gifts from God. He is here to **lead** and **guide** us to all **truth** as said in John 16:13.

We receive the Holy Spirit simply by asking God. Jesus said:

"If a son shall ask bread of any of you that is a father, will he give him a stone? Or if he ask a fish, will he for a fish give him a serpent? Or if he shall ask an egg, will he offer him a scorpion? If ye then, being evil, know how to give good gifts unto your children: how much more shall your heavenly Father give the **Holy Spirit** *to them that ask him?"*

Luke 11:11-13

God specifically sent the Holy Spirit here for **us**. Jesus knew that we needed him here. So He sent us His Spirit as the equipment that we need to function and navigate through this life. The Holy Spirit is here. Waiting, and eager to indwell God's people! Everyone who is a believer in Jesus Christ is a candidate to receive the Holy Spirit. If you haven't yet received Him *(The Holy Spirit)* or His baptism, you can ask God to fill you right now. Begin to pray and ask the Lord, you can even quote God's Word in Luke 11:11-13 back to Him in your prayer. You may also recite this small prayer that God laid on my heart for you.

"Dear Lord, I thank you so much that you've given me salvation. That you are calling me to greater understanding and knowledge of you.

I thank you Lord that you are calling me to go deeper in you. I realize God that in order for me to go deeper and to be stable, I need your Holy Spirit. Your Word says that if I ask for the Holy Spirit you will give it to me. So God, today, right now, I'm asking that you fill me with your Holy Spirit, endow me with your Holy Spirit, and baptize me with your Holy Spirit. So I believe now, that I have received what you have given me. I have received the promise from you; which is your awesome Holy Spirit. Thank you! In Jesus name, it is so; it is finished. Amen!"

— *Shalayna Janelle*

Chapter 3
Prayer

~First Fruits~

What's the first thing you do when you wake up in the morning? Some would say they get up, put their slippers on and brush their teeth. I would ask, "Do you engage God? Do you thank God? Do you pray?"

We should!

I believe in giving God our first fruits! That means when I wake up, I like to thank Jesus for allowing me to see another day. Then, I pray and read my Word (the Bible). Sometimes, I read the Bible before I pray so that I can pray God's Word. But I make it my business to give God the very first part of my day. After all, He deserves it. But as I do this faithfully, I see God's hand in my life. I see His hand all throughout the day. He is in my decision making, attitudes, reactions, speech; He directs me toward His favor and more. Believe it or not, prayer is one way we can worship God! Below are some tips on how to give God your first fruits!

#1 Acknowledge God
- Thank God for life
- Then begin to thank Him for whatever else comes to mind.

#2 Pray
- Intercession (1 Tim 2:1) (Eph 6:18)
- Listening (Zech 2:13) (Hab 2:20) (1 Kings 19:11-18)
- Worship (Ps 86:9-10) (Eph 5:20) (1 Thess 5:18)
- Petitioning (Phil 4:6) (Ps 6:9) (Ps 102:17)
- Pray God's Word (Lk 4:4) (Rom 10:11) (1 Cor 1:31)

> **Intercession** is you going to God and praying on the behalf of others. Often times, God will put a person or something in your spirit. You can intercede on the behalf of that person.

> **Listening** is when you begin to just listen to God in prayer. What you're doing is acknowledging God's sovereignty by being silent. But also you are listening to hear what He wants to speak to you. God will reveal things pertaining to your current situation, or future. It is during this time that God usually gives us instructions, insight (as well as who/what to intercede for) or even warnings.

> **Worship** is a form of prayer where you come to God simply to let Him know how much you love Him and appreciate Him. This is where you magnify, exalt, and lift God up. Lavishing Him with your love expecting nothing in return. Simply just being appreciative, grateful, in awe of the beauty of who God is and what He means to you. This can be coupled with **thanksgiving**.

Petitioning the Lord is what Philippians 4:6 refers to when it says "Let your requests be made known to God." It is ok to petition and ask of God. It just isn't the only form of prayer.

Praying the Word of God is just meditating on God's Word and making the Scriptures your prayers.

Example: "Thy word is a lamp unto my feet, and a light unto my path" (Psalm 119:105).

You could pray like this:

"Lord, I'm humble before you right now. As I am walking into this new season, I don't see what's ahead! I ask you to be a lamp unto my feet today. Please be a light unto my pathway and direct me in which way I should go. Let your way and direction be made perfectly clear to me. In Jesus' name, amen."

~Time on my hands~

We should make God a part of our everyday actions. Why not talk to God about what's going on in your life? I've found that most people say this as a cliché—"God is my best friend!" But they don't actually act like it. They don't really have conversations with the Lord. The best advice I can give about this is to talk to God as much as you can. He is the only person you can talk to who actually HAS the answer to everything: problems, situations, random questions or not so random questions. He is in control of the answers and outcomes for everyone's life! Now—that's a best friend to brag about and talk about to others! He is truly the best, best friend! Why not go to Him and converse with Him as such?

Psalm 8:4 says "What is man that thou art mindful of him?" God's desire to commune with us is so strong that the psalmist couldn't even understand why a holy God would want that much to do with us. God wants to talk to you. In fact, it brings Him joy to be *the* main person you talk to. Not the last resort after you've spoken to everyone else. It's a form of respect and putting God in His rightful place when you personally go to Him—first.

~Fasting with Prayer~

As I began to truly walk with the Lord He began to call me to fast. To some, this may sound funny or unusual. But God does call people to go on fasts. It's not a random, one time a year tradition that you have. Fasting is a valuable part of the Christian lifestyle.

So as I began to incorporate fasting into my lifestyle, I immediately saw results. Fasting and praying took me deeper with God. One of the purposes of fasting is to commune with God! It keeps you more in tune with the spiritual realm and to see in the spirit more clearly. Many times, we can fast for answers. With my experiences, God began to lead and guide me. While fasting, His Word began to jump out at me more. It was like I was literally being fed His Word and being satisfied by all of it—not left confused and unsatisfied. My biggest breakthroughs have come as a result of fasting and praying!

Quick testimony

One year, I was fasting to get closer to God. I was seeking a deeper relationship and growth in Him. While on this fast, I felt the Lord tell me to move to another apartment, so I went forward with that. When we fast we should always be listening for God to speak. I began looking around for places, and I couldn't find any that I liked or that were for the price I was willing to pay. I continued looking, praying, and fasting. The countdown was on and there were only a few days left before I had to be out of my apartment.

There was one particular city that I had not considered living in and so, I didn't even bother to search for an apartment there. I never saw myself living there. But I heard the Lord say, "Look in that city." Funny huh? So I looked, and I called this particular place. It so happened that the manager's work schedule only allowed him to receive applications after 5p.m., so I prayed and made my way over there. When I got there, He told me that there were people ahead of me and there was only one apartment available but if I still wanted to apply, I could. I felt it in my spirit that I had to apply because this was supposed to be my apartment. In response to him, I asked: "Ok, when will I know if I'm approved (because I had to be out of my apartment in about 3 days)?" He said that between sending the owner the documents and the time it would take for them to check all of the info and return them, it would take about three business days. Furthermore, they didn't process applications on weekends.

Some people wouldn't have risked cutting it that close because it had the potential to leave them without a place to live—but I knew what the Lord had told me. Even though this was a city where I never thought I would live, I knew what the Lord said and how He led me to this place. Let me add that the manager kept trying to plant seeds of doubt by saying things like, "Well I don't really know. The owners are super strict with applications, don't get your hopes up, etc". But there is nothing like knowing God and hearing what *He* has already told you and standing on it! Faith! So as I said, time was winding down—I basically had no time, and no other apartments to consider. In the natural, it totally looked like I would have had no place to stay by the time I had to leave my other apartment. Remember, though, I was still fasting, praying, and believing God. So after I left this apartment complex, I walked out of the building and noticed there was a church right across the street. They were actually in there having service—in Spanish might I add. Although they didn't speak English, it didn't matter to me. I went in, sat down, began to pray, sang to the Lord and worshiped Him in prayer. (I like to thank God in advance for what He's doing and about to do!) Then I went home. I remember having a heart of "Lord let your will be done. I just want to be in your perfect will." I'm pretty sure you know this story is going to end well because God is faithful!

Remember, there were people ahead of me for this one

apartment. I also didn't have all the time to waste because I needed to be out of my other apartment asap (by the 1st). I ended up getting a call I believe only two days later, they said I got the approval to rent the apartment if I still wanted it. Of course, I wanted it! I needed it! I was excited! I ended up working hard to move from my old place to the new place in only one morning because I had to attend a 3day revival at my church that I didn't want to miss.

Fasting gave me insight and clear direction on where God wanted me to be. Fasting takes the flesh out of the way and moves you into the spirit. That's why it is a pivotal part of a Christian's faith walk. What it also did was move the hand of the Lord. I'm one of the last people who applied for that apartment *but God* gave it to me and in time. The main point here is that I got these positive results because I was fasting and heard God's will and direction about moving to a place I didn't see myself ever living in. It wasn't about the material home. It was about getting clear and correct direction from God because that is where God needed me to be. That place was where an overflow in the spiritual and in the natural began rushing in. Within about 7-10 days of being there, I had more work coming in than I had ever experienced before. Different avenues of ministry began to be birthed. My season changed simply by one obedient move and being in the right place for the right season. I literally knew the Lord told me to move to a place I had not previously considered moving to. However, moving to that place represented moving to a new season, which changed my life and increased my growth in God.

Fasting will shift some things and have you more keen in the spirit. God responds to us when we fast. Why? Because when we're fasting, we see even more in the spiritual realm. We see even more clearly what His perfect will is for specific situations in our lives. You will see the hand of God move when you approach Him in faith while fasting. To just be able to seek God's face and get into His presence accompanied with fasting will grow our relationship with the Lord.

Fasting cultivates SUPER-natural spiritual benefits. I found myself delving into realms of God that I didn't know existed. God began to heighten my senses in Him. He brought on deeper revelation. Fresh words from God comes from fasting and praying. Knowing how to lead properly comes from fasting and praying.

Can you imagine going to a different place with God—another realm with the Lord? God will begin to give you wisdom and understanding about things in your life and things in the world. I know for me, my spirit man feels an extra dose of being in tune with God during and after a fast. My insight changes, my mindset changes. There's always an upgrade in the spirit when you fast and give that time to God! There's nothing like the immediate experiences of fasting. When you're just flowing in the spirit, no longer in just the natural experience, it's your spirit man beginning to cry out and intercede! When your natural body can't get through, your spirit man will begin to consult the Lord. Your worship begins to shift and change. What's on your mind begins to change.

When you are fasting, you are literally dying to your flesh. Your spirit man starts to take control. Taking you to a place where you begin to see things clearly. Though your natural eye may be blurry because you're hungry, it's your yielded spirit that the Holy Spirit can work through and begin to show you some things in the spirit. He starts to reveal things that you may not have been able to see before. Now, you can see them from God's perspective. It is in this time also where God can warn you about things, people, and circumstances. It is also in this place where God can begin to deal with you, work on you, and propel you from one place in the spirit to the next. We all want to see the manifestations of God! We all want to be used in that capacity. Fasting and praying is a sure way to see the manifestation of God and be used by Him.

Some people are just a fast away from a true life

changing breakthrough in certain areas of their lives. When you have a petition—petition God with fasting. God will give you answers and strategies to things that you've been seeking Him for, for a while. Once again, I believe that fasting should be a pivotal part of every true believer's life. Fasting is a form of worship and commitment. It shows that we are willing to put ourselves, desires, and the fleshly carnal nature aside to get closer to God and sup with Him.

Everyone should know that it is possible to get into that place with God and petition Him. To be able to let God take you to new realms.

Step out in faith and believe God in this area. You will see GOD results. God will take you places and show you things.

Most often, God may ask us to fast from food, but He may also ask that we include other things like not watching television or not using Facebook during the fast. God sometimes will challenge you to see if you will kill your flesh.

Temporary sacrifices create the greatest long-term harvest. I love spiritual breakthrough and advancement. Yes— material things are great and some things are needed. But the spiritual benefits we receive from fasting are what we can use to carry us through situations and make the right decisions in life.

References to a few types of fasts: (Please confirm with the Lord what HE wants you to do. Also, consult a physician if you have any concerns. Do nothing in haste or zeal!)

Fasting from food

- No food, just water for full days or a certain time period throughout the day. (Consult the Lord about the number of days/timeframes.) (Luke 4:2)
- No food, no water (Please only do this if confirmed by the Lord). Found in Exodus 34:28

& Esther 4:16.

- <u>Daniel fast:</u> Fruits and vegetables. (21 days or however long God says). This can be found in Daniel Chapter 10.

Along with fasting, you may also include abstaining from manmade pleasures.

This includes things like:

- TV
- Social media
- Shopping
- Electronics (such as video games)

When fasting use wisdom. Be led by the Lord in all things and consult a physician if you currently have health issues. Don't move in zeal or for personal glory!

<u>Helpful tips:</u>
~Journaling~
Since prayer is direct communication between you and God, you should always keep a prayer journal to track these things:

1. To write down your petitions and requests to God (along with the dates you petitioned God & the dates He answered.)
2. To write down what God speaks to you! (Instructions, how He feels about you, confirmations, etc.)

Chapter 4
Growing In God

Spending time with God is one of the greatest and most beneficial aspects of worshiping Him! By spending time with the Father, we get to learn more about Him. The more we learn about Him, the more we can trust Him and the more faith we have in Him. He also teaches us about ourselves. By spending time with God, we can propel from one dimension in the spirit to the next. Growing in God isn't predicated on your GPA or intellect. It's about being with the King!

There's a saying, "It's not who you know, it's who knows you!" This is true. We want God to know us to the point where He says "Well done thy good and faithful servant." We don't want Him to say to us "Depart from me. I never knew you." What does He even mean by I never knew you? Doesn't God know all things? Yes— God knows all things, but "knew" in this context is like the closeness between a husband and wife. In the Bible, when it talks about a man knowing his wife, it is talking about a level of intimacy. So if God says He doesn't know you, He's actually saying: "You haven't let me in. You haven't developed intimacy with me. You know of me, but you don't really know me. There are some things about me that I want to share with you. There's something I want you to experience, but you won't let me in. You won't come closer to me." It's God's desire that we grow closer to Him.

~Secret Place~

Secret: *[Adj]* Not known or seen; not meant to be known or seen by others.

[Noun] Something that is **kept** or meant to be kept unknown or **unseen** by others.

Most of us have heard people talk about the secret place with God. Many also reference the scripture Matt 6:6, to "pray in secret." It is a blessing to have a prayer room or prayer closet. If you have the means and space to make it work, you should definitely do it. But the secret place is much more than a set-aside room. It actually starts with a "set aside" you. Getting into the secret place with God is more about your heart and your life than it is an actual room.

For me personally, when I first began to really start growing in the things of the Lord, I would pray. I pretty much had set times and spontaneous times to pray and read His Word. I also would occasionally read a devotional. From that, a desire to approach God was developed. I wanted and needed to be with Him more. I began to understand that the more I was with Him, the more changed. The more I was with Him, the more I never wanted to leave His presence. The more I was with Him, the more I became like Him. My favorite experience was that I continued to hear God and know His voice. Many people always ask, "Well, how do you know God's voice?" There's no easy way to answer this. It's simply by spending "quality" time with the Lord. I put the word "quality" in quotations because it's pivotal to making sure that you are actually building your relationship with God. Not just saying "Oh, I read a scripture, I prayed a prayer—now what? How come I don't hear or know God's voice?"

Let's liken this unto a parent, best friend, or spouse.

They could put their hands over your eyes and say "guess who," and you would know exactly who it is. Not because you made a good guess but because you know your parent, best friend or spouse. You know them and their voice so well because you either **live** with them or **hang** out with them, or both.

Can I live with God?

Yes!
*"He that **dwelleth** in the secret place of the most High shall abide under the shadow of the Almighty" (Psalm 91:1)*

Dwell: [verb] **live** in or at a specified place.
Think, speak, or write at length about (a particular subject, especially one that is a **source of happiness**, anxiety, or dissatisfaction.

Can I hang out with God?

Absolutely!
Luke 10:38-42 refers to two sisters, Mary and Martha when Jesus came to their house. Mary was spending time with Jesus sitting at His feet but Martha was so worried about serving and making everything "perfect." She even asked Jesus, do you care that my sister left me alone to do the work, can you tell her to come and help me? Jesus' response was: *"Martha, Martha, thou art careful and troubled about many things. But one thing is needful: and Mary hath chosen that good part, which shall not be taken from her."* Jesus commended Mary for spending time at His feet more.

The more I lived with and hung out with God, the more we became more intimate. Intimacy led me to become sensitive to His Spirit. You know, there's a saying: "Lord, help us to hate the things that you hate; and to love the things that you love." This quickly became my reality the more Jesus and I spent time together. His presence would cover me like a blanket and ensure me that I was safe and in His perfect will for my life.

It is God's will for every believer to be intimate with Him and to continue growing in Him. Let's face it, those who are married: when you get married, the relationship doesn't stop at the vows. Even more so with Jesus! When we accept Jesus as our **personal** Lord and Savior, the relationship doesn't stop there either. It gets personal! There's work to be done on the husband's (Jesus) part and on the wife's (us) part. Honestly, we all know He keeps His end of the bargain. He doesn't fail at all at being a great husband. The question to continuously ask is, "How am I performing as a wife to my Lord?" Am I doing my normal duties? Am I going above and beyond? Or am I slacking? Am I taking and not giving? The next question should be, "Lord, what can I do better?" That's love! Love is always seeking to do better for loved ones. There's such an abundance of happiness and true freedom in Jesus when we truly begin to develop our relationships with Him.

Develop: *[verb]* grow or cause to grow and become more mature, advanced, or elaborate. Start to exist, experience, or possess.

I love how this definition uses the words **grow** and **mature**. Growth and maturity are two very important things when it comes to God. We know this by how Jesus reacted in Matt 8:26. The disciples saw Jesus perform miracles. Nevertheless, at this particular moment when the winds got heavy, and they thought they were going to sink in the ship, they quickly forgot about Jesus' miracles, His character, and His track record. Also, in Mark 9:17-20 a man in the crowd asked Jesus to cast the demon out of his son because the disciples tried and "they could not." Jesus' response was: "*O faithless generation, how long shall I be with you? How long shall I suffer you? Bring him to me?*" Jesus quickly addresses the faith of the disciples. But later, further down in verses 28 and 29, the disciples ask Jesus why they couldn't cast out that demon when they had done so before? Jesus replied by saying, "This kind can come forth by nothing, but by **PRAYER** and **FASTING**." The very essence of why one prays and fasts is to get closer to God, to spend time with Him. So based on what Jesus said to His disciples, He was making it clear to them that you may have cast out demons before but to get to this next level it takes more. It takes something else. There are more ingredients to this mix—if you want to go up you must grow up! Jesus was basically saying: "Spend time with me, I will show you some things. You will know how to operate in these situations if you spend some valuable time with me." Many people want to be used by God but very seldom do they want to grow and mature in God. God is looking for His people to make a conscious effort to get in His face.

I remember when the relationship between God and I truly started flourishing. I remember I could see the difference because I would make conscious efforts to sit with the lord. I wanted to know His heart. It wasn't a structured type of thing, it was just me and God spending some time together. Honestly, I ended up with little things that I do when I'm with Him. Things that you and Jesus do together. Things that He uses to deepen your relationship with Him. Those are the things that for the rest of my life, I will look forward to daily!

Chapter 5
The Benefits of True Worship

I fell in love with Jesus! This then caused me to run after Him like my life depended on it. Because my life *did* depend on it Where God was, I wanted to be there. Whatever God was doing, I wanted a part in it. I began to truly live for God as a wife to a husband. He was someone I had committed myself to and being faithful to Him was not a question. As I began to live and implement all that God was leading me to do (which is what I shared with you in all the previous chapters) my life began to change drastically. I soared so high in the spirit one particular year and a half because God began to really deal with me as I yielded myself to Him. NOTHING distinguishes my walk with God from anyone else's unless you don't yield to Him!

The Lord began to slowly show me things about how He wanted me to live my life based on what He wanted and didn't want me to put in my spirit. These things started with God eliminating certain TV shows. This began to keep my spirit clean. It allowed my spirit to be alert and aware of the things of God. We have to be careful of what we put in our spirits! Everything is not allowed; everything shouldn't have access to your spirit. Believe it or not, when God asks you to do or not do something, there will always be a great result that comes from your obedience.

Let me tell you a quick story: One day, God began to start changing my eating habits. It first started when He stopped me from eating fast food (fake food that you don't know what's in it, it's cooked in 5 min instead of being fresh). He allowed me to drink only tea (including iced tea) and water. That was about two years ago. By being obedient to God I went from 120lbs-106lbs. I often get wary when people try to take pills, supplements and shakes and depend on diets instead of God. Some people even fast just to lose weight. While it's a given that fasting has noticeable physical effects, I do not by any means agree with fasting for the purpose of weight loss.

Taking something holy and using it for vain purposes doesn't reap anything good at all. Jesus wants to get close to His people. Can you imagine if we come to Him and fast for a purpose other than Him, having our own agendas and He's not in it? That's a slap in the face. Fasting is for the purpose of getting closer to and growing in the Lord. If you do it for any reason other than God, you won't reap the spiritual benefits of it.

Remember, when you do what God asks of you, He'll take care of you! Every area of your life! A simple act of obedience made a noticeable change in my life. That was God! At the time, I was doing acting and entertainment fulltime. I ended up getting new headshots and those new headshots had a glow to them that I previously didn't have. I also was noticeably smaller than I was before. No, I didn't lose 300 lbs, but God did something noticeably different in my life based on what He had planned for me in upcoming seasons. I began to immediately book more roles and signed with a new agent. My career began to take off well. There's a scripture that says "The blessing of the Lord maketh rich and it addeth no sorrow with it" (Proverbs 10:22). Sometimes, the blessing of the Lord is attached to how you worship God with your life— your obedience. One small act of obedience can help you and propel you into the next step for what you are called to do. Had I not been obedient, I would have just carried on with life as usual, doing the same things I did before. I wouldn't have dropped a few pounds and needed new headshots, neither would I have booked the new roles and gotten that new agent.

Your obedience to God now, will cause you to be positioned for where God is taking you. Sometimes, it may look unnecessary to be obedient to God. Sometimes, you may not understand why the Lord is asking and requiring something of you. But when you understand that obedience is worship then, you'll look at it differently. When you understand that God knows why He does what He does and it's not up to us to figure it out. It will help you with trusting Him. I did not know the specific reasons why God was requiring those things of me when He asked. I didn't know I would reap the specific benefits that I did. I thank God for leading me to better health and wellbeing by asking me to do some things that some would call unnecessary. Our lives are about the end result. We're asked to do a thing now because God is aware of where He's taking us. He knows what He has for us so He desires to prepare us.

For instance, let's say God is trying to give you wisdom, understanding, insight, patience—things you need to properly handle what He set out for you! So, let's say, April 21, 2033, God had it set out and marked already that you were going to walk into a multi-billion-dollar company's office and make a multi-million or multi-billion-dollar deal. But all the years prior, He was trying to give you some things to help you be prepared and ready for that situation. You didn't see it, but He did. If you don't embrace the smaller things, the smaller requests from God, the smaller situations that God is trying to take you through, you won't be prepared or ready for the bigger things and opportunities He has set out for you!

So you walk into this multi-billion-dollar office for this multi-billion-dollar deal and find out you have no self-control, no understanding or knowledge, no wisdom, no patience, no insight, and no discernment. The people in the boardroom ask you, "Ok, strategically, how would you handle this?" You are stumped! You do not know how to answer. Think about it—the insight and knowledge that you could have acquired before would've helped you seal that deal. But you missed it because you didn't acquire what God needed you to. Maybe, you didn't take His requests seriously. Some people don't want to be obedient to what are the building steps of their calling! Often times, people have a mindset that situations today are just today's situations and have no direct connection with their future. But I believe, today's situations pave the way to for future harvests. You don't want to be that person who didn't want to go through what God told you to go through or sacrifice what He wanted you to sacrifice and then end up seeing how important it would have been to the calling God had for you.

Not worshiping God with our lives costs us something more than temporary sacrifices. This boardroom situation could have gone another way as well. You could have stepped into that office and made a deal that you don't know how to handle. You truly don't know how to handle all of the requirements of the deal you made. You made a deal on promises that you thought you would be able to fulfill, but in reality, you cannot fulfill them because you weren't properly grounded in what God wanted you to be first. Perhaps, integrity was one of the things God wanted to build in you, but you refused to obey so you begin to operate without integrity just to get jobs done. Can you imagine how unaligned with God's will we can be if we choose not to move with God and not to trust Him when He's trying to teach us?

Remember that everything God requests of us, takes us through or allows is for our benefit. We take these benefits with us based on what God has created and called us to do.

So the story doesn't end there! The Lord then took another thing off from my life. He told me to only drink water throughout the day and with meals. So now I drink water. No iced tea or even 100% juice etc. (unless I'm taking communion). Sometimes, I just drink hot water at night instead, for vocals. This has been over a year and a half so far.

Now brace yourself! The Lord has me now (starting this year) being vegetarian/pescetarian. A pescetarian is a person who does not eat meat but eats fish. You're talking about the same girl whose favorite food is **chicken**. I'm vegetarian. I say vegetarian more than pescetarian because God has given me the release to eat fish, but I personally have never been super fond of fish, so I only eat it once in a while. I don't say these things to lift myself up. But I say it because God will have you do what you need to do for what He has planned in your life. There are things that God is asking of us that are for our good and that will prepare us for things and situations even if we don't know they are. These things may be seasonal or lifetime sacrifices.

I understand that the most valuable thing I have in this life is my relationship with God! I understand that my obedience in life is worship to God. I choose to worship God with my life. That includes my body and what I put in it. As you grow in God, keep in mind that He is always looking for something more than the previous. How you operated, navigated, sacrificed, and worshiped Him with your life last season will change—the bar is now raised for the next season. Some say that the definition of insanity is doing the same things you did before and expecting different results. In other words, "Every fruit yielding fruit after his kind" (Gen 1:11). So what you did last season will reap last season's results. I don't know about you, but I don't want to be complacent in God. I want to grow. I want to learn. I want to experience more of Him. I don't want to hinder what God wants to do in and through me.

We have to be in a place where we are willing to go through "the go through" to get to "the get to." God wants us to be continuously moving forward in Him. He wants to take us to a place where we haven't even pictured ourselves being. We do not have the slightest clue about what God is doing behind the scenes. But praise God that our job isn't to figure it out. Our job is to trust Him with our lives so much that we fully, totally, and completely worship Him. You never have to force yourself to be a certain thing or look a certain way. If we are precise to hear God and obedient to Him, He takes care of the rest.

Let's keep our focus in the right place. I use this particular example of weight, weight loss, and vanity because it's universal. We see it all the time! It's common with both men and women. The focus is on becoming vain. The focus has become more about weight loss and body size than being healthy because we want to honor God with our temples! If God wants anything pertaining to this subject, it would be for us to be healthy. His Word tells us: "Beloved, I wish above ALL things that thou mayest prosper and be in good health; Even as thy soul prospereth"(3 John 1:2).

I wanted you to know that God can take care of everything that concerns you (Psalm 138:8). This may not be your particular issue but the moral is still the same. Seek His face, spend time with Him, and seek His will for your life, not the fads and trends of this world! It shouldn't be easier to run to things, people, and products because you trust going to those things before or instead of going to God. Your validation and answers are in Jesus Christ! God sees into your past, present, and future all at the same time. Whatever you may be facing is not bigger than Jesus! I am 100% sure that if God sees an issue, He will give His wisdom and instruction to you on how to fix that problem. There are many problems and issues that people put before God. Let's not be more focused on the cares of this world than we are the Word and will of God for our lives.

God has a result for everything—an answer for everything. When we begin to actually sit with God, talk with Him and ask Him what He desires for our lives and what changes He wants us to make in whatever season we are in, we begin to hear His heart for our lives.

Back to those instructions that God gives us in our listening prayer time. He will begin to lead you and guide you into what you need to do for **your** particular situation for that season. He has the answers! He will give you an answer for something that you may even think is little or too small. But God's Word said: "The Lord will perfect that which concerneth me" (Ps 138:8).

Since health is the example I used here in this chapter. If you've been struggling in this particular area, begin to look at things from God's perspective. With the mindset of "I desire to be healthy because my body is the temple of the Holy Spirit!" Not, "I desire to be skinny." So you are saying: "I want to do these things to please you Lord. I want to be able to be used whenever and however you choose to use me." For that reason, I'm going to take care of myself because I want to be the best version of me that I can be for God. I don't ever want to be called into the game to fail and make the team lose because I wasn't properly prepared. I want to bring my **A** game to every one of God's tasks. So I choose to take better care of myself as an act of worship to God. I put away vain desires and vain motives, and I put away trust in products—I give over my trust to God.

Bring your life (everything) and its issues to God and wait for His answer and instruction. Be willing to receive what He says. Take His instructions knowing that He knows what's best for us all. Who knows—He may ask you to do some unusual things in your life or make unusual changes in any area of your life. Sometimes, these things could be short-term, long-term or lifelong. But the focus isn't "How long do you want me to do this God?" It's being obedient and trusting that our Lord wouldn't do anything that wasn't good for us (Romans 8:28).

Your obedience and pursuit of God will take care of those things. When you are in God's perfect will, I believe it is the #1 form of true worship. You are in His perfect will when everything in your life begins to line up with all that He has for you simply because you're loving God; simply because you fell in love with Him and you want to please Him. You just begin to want more of God. Things will begin to maneuver. God will cause you to grow in Him and His ways. All of a sudden, you'll see results from the simple things God asked of you and implemented in your life, not realizing that those were the small steps that God was using. God uses small things to propel us and help grow us to become the men and women of God He needs us to be. Who knows, in the future, you may be a public speaker, preacher, working with teens or working with those recovering from drugs but you had no idea.

Example: God may have been asking or strategically trying to get you to gain confidence and helping you to be content with your testimony of being a teen mother or father and how He delivered you from depression. You may not know that three years down the line, God has it in His plans for you to be teaching young men and women about confidence and appreciating their own testimony because their past doesn't predict their future. But if you never picked up the required skills and experiences to do so (in this example confidence and deliverance from your past) you wouldn't have effectively been able to do what God really called you to do.

Our destinies and our callings are dependent on our obedience. We should always want to be in God's perfect will. If you don't know what that is just pray: *"Lord, show me your perfect will for my life. Show me your will for this season of my life."*

Look at everything God asks and requires of you as an internship with God where there are possible job offers.

Stay focused on Jesus. Stay focused on the one who knows you and created you! Your complete focus on Him will lead you to greater intimacy and relationship with Him. As well as everything He has for you.

Chapter 6
Scriptures to Use During Worship & Prayer

The following pages consist of scriptures in the categories of worship & prayer.

Use these scriptures and make them personal. When you pray, praise and have your alone time with God use these scriptures from your point of view. Saying things like "Lord I will," "Lord I know," "Lord I believe," etc. along with the scriptures. Make this personal between you and God!

"Enter into his gates with thanksgiving, and into his courts with praise: be thankful unto him, and bless his name."
Psalm 100:4

"Set your affection on things above, not on things on the earth."
Col 3:2

"But the hour cometh, and now is, when the true worshippers shall worship the Father in spirit and in truth: for the Father seeketh such to worship him. God is a spirit: and they that worship him must worship him in spirit and in truth."
John 4: 23, 24

"Thou art worthy, O Lord, to receive glory and honor and power: for thou hast created all things, and for thy pleasure they are and were created."
Revelation 4:11

"And Jesus answered and said unto him, 'Get thee behind me, Satan: for it is written, Thou shalt worship the Lord thy God, and him only shalt thou serve.'"
Luke 4:8

"Wherefore we receiving a kingdom which cannot be moved, let us have grace, whereby we may serve God acceptably with reverence and Godly fear: for our God is a consuming fire."
Hebrews 12: 28, 29

"And I John saw these things, and heard them. And when I had heard and seen, I fell down to worship before the feet of the angel which shewed me these things. Then saith he unto me, 'see thou do it not: for I am thy fellow-servant, and of thy brethren the prophets, and of them

which keep the sayings of this book: worship God.'"
Revelation 22:8, 9

"I beseech you therefore, brethren, by the mercies of God, that ye present your bodies a living sacrifice, holy, acceptable unto God, which is your reasonable service."
Romans 12:1

"And be not conformed to this world: but be ye transformed by the renewing of your mind, that ye may prove what is that good, and acceptable, and perfect, will of God."
Romans 12:2

"Sing unto the LORD, all the earth; shew forth from day to day his salvation. Declare his glory among the heathen; his marvelous works among all nations. For great is the LORD, and greatly to be praised: he also is to be feared above all gods. For all the Gods of the people are idols: but the LORD made the heavens. Glory and honor are in his presence; strength and gladness are in his place. Give unto the LORD, ye kindreds of the people, give unto the Lord Glory and strength. Give unto the LORD glory due unto his name: bring an offering, and come before him: worship the LORD in the beauty of holiness, Fear before him, all the earth: the world also shall be stable, that it be not moved. Let the heavens be glad, and let the earth rejoice: and let men say among the nations, The LORD reigneth. Let the sea roar, and the fullness thereof: let the fields rejoice, and all that is therein."
1 Chronicles 16:23-32

"The LORD reigneth; let the people tremble: he sitteth between the cherubims; let the earth be moved. The LORD is great in zion; and he is high above all the people. Let them praise thy great and terrible name; for it is holy. The king's strength also loveth judgment; thou dost establish equity, thou executes judgment and righteousness in Jacob. Exalt ye the LORD our God, and worship at his footstool; for he is holy. Moses and Aaron among his priests, and Samuel among them that call upon his name; they called upon the LORD, and he answered them. He spake unto them in the cloudy pillar: they kept his testimonies, and the ordinance that he gave them. Thou answeredst them, O LORD our God: thou wast a God that forgavest them, though thou tookest vengeance of their inventions. Exalt the Lord our God, and worship at his holy hill; for the LORD our God is holy."

Psalm 99

Scriptures Regarding Prayer

"I will therefore that men pray everywhere, lifting up holy hands, without wrath and doubting."

1 Timothy 2:8

"But ye, beloved, building up yourselves on your most holy faith, praying in the Holy Ghost."

Jude 1:20

"And he spake a parable unto them to this end, that men ought always to pray, and not to faint."

Luke 18:1

"According to the eternal purpose which he purposed in Christ Jesus our Lord: In whom we have boldness and access with confidence by the faith of him."

Ephesians 3:11-12

"Praying always with all prayer and supplication in the Spirit, and watching thereunto with all perseverance and supplication for all saints."

Ephesians 6:18

"Rejoice in the Lord alway: and again I say, Rejoice. Let your moderation be known unto all men. The Lord is at hand. Be careful for nothing; but in every thing by prayer and supplication with thanksgiving let your requests be made known unto God. And the peace of God, which passeth all understanding, shall keep your hearts and minds through Christ Jesus. Finally, brethren, whatsoever things are true, whatsoever things are honest, whatsoever things are just, whatsoever things are pure, whatsoever things are lovely, whatsoever things are of good report; if there be any virtue, and if there be any praise, think on these things. Those things, which ye have both learned, and received, and heard, and seen in me, do: and the God of peace shall be with you."
Philippians 4:4-9

"Continue in prayer, and watch in the same with thanksgiving."
Colossians 4:2

"Pray without ceasing."
1 Thessalonians 5:17

"For the word of God is quick, and powerful, and sharper than any two-edged sword, piercing even to the dividing asunder of soul and spirit, and of the joints and marrow, and is a discerner of the thoughts and intents of the heart. Neither is there any creature that is not manifest in his sight: but all things are naked and opened unto the eyes of him with whom we have to do. Seeing then that we have a great high priest, that is passed into the heavens, Jesus the Son of God, let us hold fast our profession. For we have not an high priest which cannot be touched with the feeling of our infirmities; but was in all points tempted like as we are, yet without sin. Let us therefore come boldly unto the throne of grace, that we may obtain mercy, and find grace to help in time of need."

Hebrews 4:12-16

"Confess your faults one to another, and pray one for another, that ye may be healed. The effectual fervent prayer of a righteous man availeth much."
James 5:16

Epilogue

Remember the #1 form of worship is being in God's perfect will for **your** life! Put everything aside to run for what God wants you to do. Run for the purposes that He has created you accomplish in this life. He has created you for a specific purpose. — yes you! When you can lay all of you down, lay everything aside and just run whole heartedly on the vision that He set forth for you to complete it affects your surroundings, actions, and those you choose to have in your life. When we can worship God with this very life of ours then the 20 minutes of worship during the church service can be genuine. Because your worship isn't predicated on music. Your worship isn't an emotional experience. It's dependent on how you feel about God. It has become your lifestyle! It's true worship! This is what we're aiming for!

The Truth
(Author Statement)

Had I not lived out what I am writing to you in this book, I would have probably never written it because I wouldn't have had anything to share with you all.

This is the first book that I am releasing. Never in my life did I see myself as an author, actress, singer/songwriter and preacher; I didn't think writing books was for someone like me. I didn't think twice about things like this. Honestly, I didn't see God having a need to call me into this sector—this field. But because I was obedient to God, followed where He led me and I was in alignment with even the small things He asked me to do, I was maneuvered into this place where He finally said: "Ok I need you to write this book." And I was able to. Had I dodged all of the things that God was trying to teach me; had I dodged all of the requests that He initially gave me to do this ministry of writing books wouldn't have been birthed. There would have been no substance.

The thing that really propelled me into writing this book was the fact that the Lord asked me to give up my job/career pursuit (God asked me to stop pursuing acting). That was one of the last big things He required of me before He shifted me into this new place of writing books. I was obedient even though acting was something I loved since I was about 5 years old. "Stop working for this new season I'm bringing you into and focus on full-time ministry." I knew God was speaking to me. Not knowing, if He would bring me into the acting field in another season, in a different way, I still went with His lead. I gave it up! Why? Because His plan means more to me.

In my head, full-time ministry was…"OK, I'm a singer/songwriter and preacher. So I'm just going to continue to focus on preaching and putting another album together." I didn't worry about bills and finances because the Lord is and has always shown Himself to be a provider for me. That's my Daddy, I trust Him to provide. Bills are always taken care of (Philippians 4:19, 20).

So I obeyed! With a slingshot of faith in the Lord, I walked into this new season ready to perform like David did toward Goliath. Not realizing that in that time, God was going to commission me to write books. That He was going to stir up my spirit about it so much that I had to get on it. I had to do it. God birthed a new avenue of ministry in my life through obedience! Committing to God as I wrote about in this book will cause you to say yes to the beautiful unknown and be able to live out and experience what God has in store for you. It was a blessing to minister to people while working in Hollywood as an actor. So I want to encourage you that everyone has a calling into ministry full-time in some capacity even on your jobs, in your homes, and at the grocery store. We should all be a light wherever we are! God is by no means requiring everyone to leave their job. He's simply requiring your obedience.

That is why I believe it is pivotal to get to a place of "Lord I love you 'sooo' much! I believe you. I believe you so much that I receive what you say to me and ask of me. And because of that, I will do anything for you God!"

I am a living witness that anything can strategically move you from one place to the next, having no idea that that's what it was going to do. One place to the next, one step to the next until you get to the place—those divine places where God needs you to be. And this place that I am at—me having written this book was a divine place that God needed me to be. I'm grateful, blessed, and humbled to be used by God to share this with you! Always remember to lift up the name of Jesus in all you do!

"Looking unto Jesus; The AUTHOR and FINISHER of our faith" (Heb 12:2).

Take Action!
Steps to truly living a worship-filled life!
31 Days of Worship

DEVOTION WORKBOOK

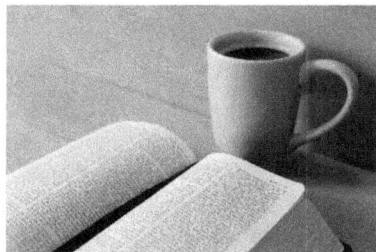

"The focus is Jesus! If Jesus can be our focus things fall into purpose; God's will is done in our lives, we become God's will and begin to boldly live out that will." - Shalayna Janelle

DAY 1

"Thou art worthy, O Lord, to receive glory and honor and power: for thou hast created all things, and for thy pleasure they are and were created."
Revelation 4:11

The twenty-four elders in this scripture understood who God was. They also understood why they were created and acknowledged Him as the Creator of ALL things. Because of this, they worshiped God by telling Him that He was worthy to receive **glory**, **honor,** and **power.**

PRAYER

Today Lord, I will take time out to understand who you are and why I was created. I ask that you show me ways to glorify, honor you and show your power.
In Jesus' name, Amen.

Day 1 Worksheet/Notes

How were you able to apply this to your life today?

How were you able to see God in a new way?

Notes

DAY 2

"Enter into his gates with thanksgiving, and into his courts with praise: be thankful unto him, and bless his name."
Psalm 100:4

It seems that more often than not, people go to God to pray for everything they want. Prayer has become a hotline for "give me" requests. Wouldn't it be great to go into prayer with a heart of thanksgiving before anything else, just thanking God?

Throughout life, you may not see or feel like you are blessed or have anything to be thankful for. But you do! God has given you another day of life, good health, food, and most importantly salvation. Take time to review what God has done for you naturally and spiritually.

PRAYER

Today Lord, as I approach you to pray, I will remember all that you have done for me. Thanking you for everything even what may seem small. Help me to appreciate you, salvation, and all the daily blessings you shower me with. No blessing from you is too small.
In Jesus' name. Amen.

Day 2 Worksheet/Notes

How were you able to apply this to your life today?

How were you able to see God in a new way?

Notes

DAY 3

"And he cometh unto the disciples, and findeth them asleep, and saith unto Peter, What, could ye not watch with me one hour? Watch and pray, that ye enter not into temptation: the spirit indeed is willing, but the flesh is weak."
Matthew 26:40, 41

Jesus needed His disciples to pray with Him in the garden of Gethsemane. He knew that danger was coming. This was just before He was to be taken away to be crucified. When He saw that they were sleeping instead of praying He asked them: "Couldn't you watch with me for only one hour?"

Praying is a pivotal part of our faith walk. How often do you find yourself wanting to sleep rather than pray? Or wanting to do something else rather than pray? Here, Jesus makes it clear to us that praying can show us when danger is going to come. It can keep us from falling into temptation.

Sometimes, you may not feel like praying but ask God to give you the strength to move past what your flesh wants and still pray.

PRAYER

Thank you Lord, for showing me the significance of prayer. I see now that prayer can shift situations. So whenever you call me to pray, I will pray whether I feel tired or busy. Thank you for revealing this to me.
In Jesus' name. Amen.

Day 3 Worksheet/Notes

How were you able to apply this to your life today?

How were you able to see God in a new way?

Notes

DAY 4

"I have set the LORD always before me: because he is at my right hand, I shall not be moved."
Psalm 16:8

How easy is it to say I trust God? Very easy! However, I find that most people find it hard to actually apply it. The psalmist declares that he will not be moved. That's a bold statement. What does he mean? He means that no matter what comes his way; no matter the circumstances or what things look like, he's going to stay firmly planted in the Lord.

You should too! God has always been God in your life and has always protected and come through for you. His track record with you is 100%!!! His faithfulness to you alone is enough to trust Him wholeheartedly. When you trust Him you can stand firm and not be moved.

PRAYER

Lord, I acknowledge that you are Alpha and Omega. So I set you above ALL in my life. I will stand on your promises. I will not doubt you or be swayed out of your will and presence.
In Jesus' name. Amen.

Day 4 Worksheet/Notes

How were you able to apply this to your life today?

How were you able to see God in a new way?

Notes

DAY 5

"Therefore my heart is glad, and my glory rejoiceth: my flesh also rest in hope."
Psalm 16:9

Things happen in life that try to steal our joy and happiness. Maybe a rude boss, disobedient children, fallout with a friend, argument with a spouse or financial issues. Whatever the case, God is looking for His people to get to a place where their joy isn't dependent on "perfect" situations. But it's an unshakable joy straight from God!

If we walk around with this kind of joy, others around us will see. They will begin to want what we have. Believe it or not, others see the glory of God in our lives and admire it. Give them another reason to be drawn to Jesus.

PRAYER

Today Lord, because I know you and trust you, I choose to be glad and rejoice in you! I release all stress and anxiety to you. I will keep my mind focused on walking in the spirit. I will rest knowing that you have everything under control.
In Jesus' name. Amen.

Day 5 Worksheet/Notes

How were you able to apply this to your life today?

How were you able to see God in a new way?

Notes

DAY 6

"Shew me thy ways, O LORD; teach me thy paths."
Psalm 25:4

Ever feel like you just don't know what to do? What your next turn should be? Or how you should handle things?

Go to Jesus! Turn to Him!

The most useful wisdom is hidden in God. The clearest and most precise instructions come from the Lord. The psalmist asking God to **show** him His ways and **teach** him His paths was a humble step. He had already taken a step in the right direction by seeking God! Sometimes, we have to sit at Jesus' feet and ask Him to teach us how to be more like Him and what paths we need to take that will keep us in Him?

PRAYER

"Lord, I don't know what to do in this particular season. But I know the best thing is to ask you to show me your ways. I want to move where you move and act how you act. Reveal to me your ways and your will so I can become what it is that you want me to be. Show me your path so I can walk in it.
In Jesus' name. Amen.

Day 6 Worksheet/Notes

How were you able to apply this to your life today?

How were you able to see God in a new way?

Notes

DAY 7

"And unto the angel of the church in Smyrna write; these things saith the first and the last, which was dead, and is alive."
Revelation 2:8

Does your life reflect **life**? Does your life look **lively**? Can people tell by your life that you have God **living** inside of you?

Contrary to what some may say, you can't reflect a **living God** while having a **dead spirit**. By dead spirit, I mean—having no joy, peace, hope, happiness, faith, never looking on the bright side.

Wait a minute! Now do you see how important it is that people know our God is living? The difference between Jesus and false gods is that our God is real and ALIVE! If we are projecting all things contrary to life, how would anyone be drawn by our witness? So we as followers of Christ must look like Him and project who HE is. He is love, peace, joy, happiness, life, and medicine to our bones!

PRAYER

"Lord, I don't want to bear false witness of who you truly are!
If there is any area of my life that is projecting you in a bad or false light, please reveal it to me so that I can see it and make changes to honor you.
In Jesus' name. Amen.

Day 7 Worksheet/Notes

How were you able to apply this to your life today?

How were you able to see God in a new way?

Notes

DAY 8

"Lead me in thy truth, and teach me: for thou art the God of my salvation; on thee do I wait all the day."
Psalm 25:5

Being **led**, **taught** and **waiting** sometimes, seems treacherous! Aaaaahhh! Especially to those who are "do-it-yourselfers." Those who are used to getting things done themselves sometimes have a hard time being led, taught, and definitely waiting.

God wants us all to not be dependent on ourselves. Having God lead us is a must because He knows the way. Having Him teach us is essential because our intellect is very small compared to His knowledge of life and everything else.

Waiting on God is absolutely needed. In times of waiting, we're usually being prepared and equipped for a future task. As we wait on God, we develop a true relationship of trust with Him. We trust Him and He trusts us.

PRAYER

Lord, there is a lot I need to learn daily as I grow in you. I surrender to your truth. If there is anything in my life or path that is half-truth, falsified, and flat out not true, please show it to me. I want you to teach me. Even if it's uncomfortable I'll patiently wait on you. I'll wait knowing that you are the Master and the Creator of time. You created my destiny and you never run late.
In Jesus' name. Amen.

Day 8 Worksheet/Notes

How were you able to apply this to your life today?

How were you able to see God in a new way?

Notes

DAY 9

"And these are the singers, chief of the fathers of the Levites, who remaining in the chambers were free. For they were employed in that work day and night."
1 Chronicles 9:33, 34

Do you want to be employed by God? You already are! This scripture shows us that these people were employed to worship God—not in a "pay to play" kind of way but with sincere hunger and motive to worship God. Like the prophetess Anna, they also worshiped day and night.

You're employed by God too! As the body of Christ, our job description is to glorify the Lord, tell others about Jesus, make disciples and most of all show and walk in love to name a few. You may have never looked at your life as a form of employment to God. But from here on out you should.

PRAYER

Lord, wow! I am an employee of the Most High God! My qualification was accepting you Jesus Christ as my Lord and Savior. I dedicate my daily tasks to you. What you require of me as well as my commitments, I will do in an excellent spirit.
In Jesus' name. Amen.

Day 9 Worksheet/Notes

How were you able to apply this to your life today?

How were you able to see God in a new way?

Notes

DAY 10

"His lord said unto him, Well done, good and faithful servant; thou hast been faithful over a few things, I will make thee ruler over many things; enter thou into the joy of thy lord."
Matthew 25:23

Have you ever felt like you were ready for a promotion? Do you feel you've been in this position too long and you want to be upgraded? Well, promotion comes with a lot of responsibilities. One of the greatest responsibilities that Jesus wrote about was **faithfulness**. He commended the servant who was faithful and did his best with the initial task he was given. In order to be promoted, we have to do our current jobs well. Let's ask ourselves: "Am I giving my best to the task at hand?" "Have I been responsible with what you've blessed me with?"

Remember the Day 9 devotional—you are employed by God! Let's strive to work as unto the Lord in every task we have here on earth. Being outstanding employees in the workforce make us outstanding employees for God! God sees what we do and is willing to reward us. If we are faithful in the little we may have now, He will make us rulers over much!

PRAYER

Lord, I'm committed to being faithful to what I have now because I am grateful. I know the more you can trust me with, the more you can bless me with. Thank you Lord!
In Jesus' name. Amen.

Day 10 Worksheet/Notes

How were you able to apply this to your life today?

How were you able to see God in a new way?

Notes

DAY 11

"What man is he that feareth the LORD? Him shall he teach in the way that he shall choose. His soul shall dwell at ease; and his seed shall inherit the earth."
Psalm 25:12, 13

Ease: [noun] absence of difficulty or effort
[verb] make (something unpleasant, painful, or intense) less serious or severe).

Many people would love to be at ease in the situations they are facing. What does the psalmist mean when he says that those who fear the Lord shall be at ease in their souls?

What are some of the things keeping you from being at ease?

According to this scripture, the fear of the Lord (reverencing God, knowing God) will help with that. Have you truly experienced just knowing who Jesus is? His character can show us that He is faithful, trustworthy, loving, unforgetful, forgiving, and our provider. Just knowing those few things about our Lord can show us that we have nothing in life to be worried about. God will take care of everything concerning those who fear Him. Our souls can be at ease. Having no worries, being careful for nothing, we can rest assured in God's sovereignty alone.

PRAYER

Thank you Jesus, for being sovereign! Your character is a roadmap for me to trust you! Help me to get to know you better so I may trust you better.
In Jesus' name. Amen.

Day 11 Worksheet/Notes

How were you able to apply this to your life today?

How were you able to see God in a new way?

Notes

DAY 12

"And if it seem evil unto you to serve the LORD, choose you this day whom ye will serve; whether the gods which your fathers served that were on the other side of the flood, or the gods of the Amorites, in whose land ye dwell: but as for me and my house, we will serve the LORD."
Joshua 24:15

Daily, many things get thrown at us hoping to steal our attention and focus. What we choose to focus on the most is what we've made our god. Take this time to reflect on what you give the most of your time, thoughts, and energy to. If the answer is Jesus, then Praise the Lord!!! If the answer is something other than Him then you have to do some recalculating.

Remember (Yahweh, the I Am, Jesus) is our God. He said we shall have no other gods before Him. If you've noticed something that is getting more of your time than God. Ask yourself this question: "Is this (person, place or thing) worth me not giving God His due glory and time?"

PRAYER

Lord, you are the only God. The only true God! I adore you! I will remember to put you in your rightful place. Oh God you deserve all my attention, affection, and praise. I will not give your high position to another!
In Jesus' name. Amen.

Day 12 Worksheet/Notes

How were you able to apply this to your life today?

How were you able to see God in a new way?

Notes

DAY 13

"Bless the LORD, O my soul: and all that is within me, bless his holy name."
Psalm 103:1

This is one of my favorite scripture verses. It's an awesome verse to meditate on! To think about honoring God with every fiber of our being just takes me into the presence of God. Reading and speaking this verse sparks something in me every time. Why? Well, because this is the perfect example of unconditional love and worship to God. Your heart is so fixed on Him that everything that is in your makeup aligns and says, "I will bless God's holy name—no matter how I feel, I will bless your name God because you are GOD."

To love God truly for who He is allows our hearts to want to please Him in everything we do. Our hearts cry should always be: "Lord, I want to bless your name with all that is within me."

PRAYER

Lord, you are so good to me! I want everything that is within me to bless your holy name. Give me the passion and fire to be able to live this out daily. Thank you Lord!
In Jesus' name. Amen.

Day 13 Worksheet/Notes

How were you able to apply this to your life today?

How were you able to see God in a new way?

Notes

DAY 14

"Let integrity and uprightness preserve me; for I wait on thee."
Psalm 25:21

Integrity is one of the main characteristics that unbelievers look for in a proclaimed Christian. As followers of Christ, we should be showing it.

Little white lies, cheating on tests and being hypocritical are things that the world says are ok. They try to convince themselves and each other that those types of behaviors are "not so bad."

If we are followers of Christ, He is our example. Did Jesus ever lie to us or anyone else? Did He ever cheat, steal or act hypocritically? Did Jesus ever throw away the fruits of the spirit for self-pleasure?

Let's evaluate every time we are faced with a decision and choose to stand for integrity, uprightness, and righteousness in Jesus Christ.

PRAYER

Today Lord, I'm going to start evaluating my actions! I choose to walk in integrity. For you are the God of integrity. Help my actions to be upright. Thank you Lord!
In Jesus' name. Amen.

Day 14 Worksheet/Notes

How were you able to apply this to your life today?

How were you able to see God in a new way?

Notes

DAY 15

"Finally, brethren, whatsoever things are true, whatsoever things are honest, whatsoever things are just, whatsoever things are pure, whatsoever things are lovely, whatsoever things are of good report; if there be any virtue, and if there be any praise, think on these things."
Philippians 4:8

The human mind likes to try triathlons. It races and races and tries to give those susceptible a nervous breakdown. It's human nature to act opposite of what God wants. That's why having the Holy Spirit keeps us from submitting to the flesh and human nature.

Jesus told us not to take thought for tomorrow, Paul reassures us of the same thing a couple of verses above in Phil 4:6. Many will tell you that it's normal to be anxious and have anxiety. Jesus and Paul show us otherwise. With the Holy Spirit, you can live free from anxious thoughts!

Again I ask you, What are you worrying about? Your Father is a King! He controls everything and will not harm you. Trust in the Lord and anxiety will have no place to live in your head.

PRAYER

Thank you Jesus, I know you're my King! I shall not want for anything. Lead me to truly understand what this means. Free me from anxious controlling thoughts. Thank you Lord! In Jesus' name. Amen.

Day 15 Worksheet/Notes

How were you able to apply this to your life today?

How were you able to see God in a new way?

Notes

DAY 16

"But seek ye first the kingdom of God, and his righteousness; and all these things shall be added unto you."
Matthew 6:33

We grow up with ambitions, desires, and goals. Then we have a head-on collision with Jesus Christ and our lives change. For some, the ambition and desire to move ahead for their own benefit are still hidden within. Their motivation to achieve is still for their own glory—not God's.

We have to remember, we are now part of God's kingdom. We've been employed. When the Bible says, "Seek ye first the kingdom of God" it is a reminder that our goal is putting Jesus' name out there, not our own. We should be building God's kingdom, not our own! Our Lord is so merciful that He says that if we seek His kingdom first, He will then add all the other things to us. If you help build God's house, He'll supply for yours!

PRAYER

Lord, thank you for your reminder of your will for my life! Today, I'm making a commitment to help build your kingdom, not my own. Show me ways that I can build for your name and better serve you!
In Jesus' name. Amen.

Day 16 Worksheet/Notes

How were you able to apply this to your life today?

How were you able to see God in a new way?

Notes

DAY 17

"I will lift up mine eyes unto the hills, from whence cometh my help. My help cometh from the LORD, which made heaven and earth."
Psalm 121:1, 2

Often times, people feel alone and abandoned. They feel as though they have no one to count on. To them, it seems as though when they need someone the most that is the time when everyone is gone or occupied.

The psalmist puts things into perspective. What can man do for you that God can't? What control does man have that God doesn't have? When friends are busy God is there, He's our help. Since He is always available, He's the one you should go to first.

Never feel alone just because you don't have lots of people around you. Never feel alone because someone may not understand you. Look to the hills, that's where your help is. From the God who made EVERYTHING! What can't He do for you? He surely can be your help, comforter, and friend! No time is an inappropriate time. You're always on His schedule!

PRAYER

Lord, when I need help I will look to you. You know my desires. I'm not alone because you said you will never leave me nor forsake me. Thank you!
In Jesus' name. Amen.

Day 17 Worksheet/Notes

How were you able to apply this to your life today?

How were you able to see God in a new way?

Notes

DAY 18

"The earth is the LORD's, and the fullness thereof; the world, and they that dwell there in."
Psalm 24:1

Have you ever been in a place where you felt "God doesn't see me" "God how are you going to get me out of this?" "How are you going to work this one out for me?" I learned that it's not our job to figure things out. The entire earth and its contents belong to God. Of course, you can't see a way out, but **He can** because He can see everything in this earth all at once. What you do know is who God is and what He's **already** done for you. Remember that undefeated track record of 100%. You know He hasn't lost yet and never will. It's your job to rest in that—not to do God's job.

PRAYER

Lord, you know everything! All of my situations, obstacles, and more. I will rest in knowing that you have never failed me and never will. I will spend more time thanking you in advance for future victories. Thank you Lord!
In Jesus' name. Amen.

Day 18 Worksheet/Notes

How were you able to apply this to your life today?

How were you able to see God in a new way?

Notes

DAY 19

"And be renewed in the spirit of your mind."
Ephesians 4:23

"And be not conformed to this world: but be ye transformed by the renewing of your mind, that ye may prove what is that good, and acceptable, and perfect, will of God."
Romans 12:2

When we come to Christ, we must allow Him to change and renew our minds. Have you done this? If yes, do you continue to do this?

The scripture says that transformation is by renewing your mind. Renewing means constant change for the better. It's not a onetime "ah-ha" moment when you no longer have to apply this scripture. This is a constant feeding of your spirit/mind with the Scriptures daily.

As you take in the Scriptures, the Holy Spirit allows it to renew our minds. That's how true lasting transformation comes.

PRAYER

Lord, transform my mind daily as I meditate on your Word.
Teach, correct, and rebuke me so that I think and become
more like you. This is my heart's desire!
In Jesus' name. Amen.

Day 19 Worksheet/Notes

How were you able to apply this to your life today?

How were you able to see God in a new way?

Notes

DAY 20

"Set your affection on things above, not on things on earth."
Colossians 3:2

As our minds are renewed, slowly our priorities change. We become more delighted with the things of God rather than earthly pleasures. Long term benefits become our focus.

For example, growing in the spirit will begin to carry more weight than becoming a partner at the law firm. Secondly, God's abundance of love for you and who He says you are will mean more to you than being in the popular cliques.

The point is, that the things of eternal value will have a larger place in your life as your affections continue to be on things above.

PRAYER

Thank you Lord, for beginning to transform me! Take me to the place where I become engulfed in the things above. Give me a clear perspective of what's important; what carries eternal value and what does not. Thank you Lord!
In Jesus' name. Amen.

Day 20 Worksheet/Notes

How were you able to apply this to your life today?

How were you able to see God and life in a new way?

Notes

DAY 21

"Then he said unto them, Go your way, eat the fat, and drink the sweet, and send portions unto them for whom nothing is prepared: for this day is holy unto our LORD: Neither be ye sorry; For the joy of the LORD is your strength."
Nehemiah 8:10

Wow! It's amazing to think about what this verse is actually saying.

Joy: [noun] a feeling of great pleasure and happiness.
In essence, when God is joyful. When we do things that please God and bring Him joy we're strengthened.
Strength: [noun] the quality or state of being strong, in particular. A good beneficial **quality** or **attribute** of a person or thing.
Often times, we're asked what are our strengths. People see strengths as things like boldness, generosity, love, organization, etc. We can now add to the list "the joy of the LORD." Even though people may look at us funny we can say: "Yes! The joy of the LORD is my strength!"

PRAYER

Lord, I love you! Above all else, I want to see you happy, joyous and pleased with me. Show me today what I can do to bring you joy!
In Jesus' name. Amen.

Day 21 Worksheet/Notes

How were you able to apply this to your life today?

How were you able to see God in a new way?

Notes

DAY 22

"But now ye also put off all these; anger, wrath, malice, blasphemy, filthy communication out of your mouth."
Colossians 3:8

I've heard the saying "God knows my heart" numerous times as people try to justify their sinful, ungodly actions and speech. This verse shows us that those things are not justifiable and should be put off.

God never wants us to be bitter and angry, those are characteristics of the Devil. Neither is it in Christian character to have filthy/foul speech. What we speak according to the Bible comes from our hearts (Matt 12:34, Luke 6:45), for example, cursing/ swearing, gossip, slander, dirty jokes, etc.

We must make sure that we have totally surrendered all areas of our lives to the Holy Spirit. Jesus made it clear that we cannot represent Him while participating in things that are the opposite of His character and commands.

PRAYER

Lord, I surrender my emotions, character, and speech to you today. If you find anything in my vocabulary that is not like you cleanse my speech to reflect how a child of the Most High God should speak. Thank you Lord!
In Jesus' name. Amen.

Day 22 Worksheet/Notes

How were you able to apply this to your life today?

How were you able to see God in a new way?

Notes

DAY 23

"And to the angel of the church in Philadelphia write; These things sayeth he that is holy, he that is true, he that hath the key of David, that openeth, and no man shutteth; and shutteth, and no man openeth."
Revelation 3:7

Some of us are petitioning God for open doors. While that is a great thing to ask of Him. Let's first consider from all angles why He may not comply:

1. Maybe blessed doors are not opening for us because there are some doors that need to be closed. You may not even realize there are open doors in your life that are hindering you—they need to be closed. Ask God: "Is there an open door in my life preventing me from walking in my fullness in you?"

2. Also, is there a door that you haven't walked through that God has opened for you? Sometimes, even stepping into the new is scary for some. But if God opened it—He has already aligned things and prepared you for it. Most importantly, if God opened it, no man can shut it!

PRAYER

Lord, you can do for me what I cannot do for myself. You have the key to every door in my life. Open the doors you need me to walk through. Shut every door that is not in your plan for my life. Give me the strength to walk into and walk away. I trust your decisions for my life. Thank you Lord!
In Jesus' name. Amen.

Day 23 Worksheet/Notes

How were you able to apply this to your life today?

How were you able to see God in a new way?

Notes

DAY 24

"He that dwelleth in the secret place of the most high shall abide under the shadow of the Almighty."
Psalm 91:1

God's secret place isn't a secret to those who allow Him to take them there. This is a place where you and God can become one. The more you spend time in this place with God the closer you become. Ask God to take you to the secret place where there's safety, comfort, protection, love, and friendship. His shadow alone can heal our hurts, pains, and offenses. It can add joy, peace and an overflowing abundance of love to our hearts!

PRAYER

Lord Jesus, daily as I pray and step into the secret place with you, let your shadow cover me, protect me, and engulf me with your presence and an awareness of you. I want to experience all that you have for me.
Thank you Lord!
In Jesus' name. Amen.

Day 24 Worksheet/Notes

How were you able to apply this to your life today?

How were you able to see God in a new way?

Notes

DAY 25

"For the kingdom of God is not in word, but in power."
1 Corinthians 4:20

It's easy to get set in a routine. Let's face it, most people are. One way God's people get set in routines is by being ok with talking about being Christians and not walking in the **power** of a Christian. What is the power? Mark 16:17,18 lists that we will cast out demons, speak with new tongues, take up serpents, if we were to drink something deadly, it wouldn't harm us, and we shall lay our hands on the sick, and they shall recover.

Never be satisfied with just talking the talk without demonstration. God's real movement in your life should be shown. There should be some tangible evidence in your daily life that shows the power of God! Peter was a glory carrier. He walked by people and his very shadow healed them. I told God, "I want to be a glory carrier. Anyone can talk a good talk but as you said, your kingdom isn't about talking a good game— it's about **power,** show your power through my life!" And He has— daily!

Are you allowing God to demonstrate His power through you?

PRAYER

Dear Lord, I want to carry your glory. I don't want to settle for anything less than showing your power to your people and those who may not know you. Show me what I must do to be a glory carrier.
In Jesus' name. Amen.

Day 25 Worksheet/Notes

How were you able to apply this to your life today?

How were you able to see God in a new way?

Notes

DAY 26

"And he saith unto them, Follow me, and I will make you fishers of men."
Matthew 4:19

Peter and Andrew two of Jesus' disciples already had occupations. They were **fishermen**! Then Jesus came along and said, "Follow me, I will make you **fishers of men**."

God has a funny way of using what we know to propel us into our calling. A calling that will bring Him total glory. Your earthly occupation, hobbies, or talents may just be the foreshadowing of what God really wants you to do. As the two fishermen were, be open and willing to drop the old for the new. God will call and lead you into the direction He has for you. Simply continue to work in excellence. When you've acquired the needed skills and reached the divinely appointed time, God will use them for His glory!

PRAYER

Dear Lord, you are strategic in how you work. As the two disciples did, I will work in excellence at all that you have given me so that you may at any time use me for your glory. Thank you Lord!
In Jesus' name. Amen.

Day 26 Worksheet/Notes

How were you able to apply this to your life today?

How were you able to see God in a new way?

Notes

DAY 27

"Put on therefore, as the elect of God, holy and beloved, bowels of mercies, kindness, humbleness of mind, meekness, longsuffering; forbearing one another, and forgiving one another, if any man have a quarrel against any: even as Christ forgave you, so also do ye. And above all these things put on charity, which is the bond of perfectness."
Colossians 3:12-14

Let's talk about humility. God taught me humility in many different ways. But one particular instance was a time when people I love (in the church) came up against me. Speaking and bearing false witness about me based on their feelings and what they thought was true.

Well, as I said, I LOVE those people and also respect them. I knew they were wrong, but I apologized to them. Sometimes, God will have you do this no matter if you are right. That's where humility came into play. I knew I was hurt by their false witness but instead of holding a grudge and walking in unforgiveness, I shared my heart with the Lord, and I knew that He would deal with them. God will reveal the truth. He comforted me in the situation. But most of all extreme humility was exercised and developed.

PRAYER

Dear Lord, show me ways that I can exercise humility! Allow me to be humble and let you fight for me! Let no unforgiveness harbor in my heart. I will forgive because you've forgiven me. Thank you Lord!
In Jesus' name. Amen.

Day 27 Worksheet/Notes

How were you able to apply this to your life today?

How were you able to see God in a new way?

Notes

DAY 28

"And let us run with patience the race that is set before us. Looking unto Jesus the author and finisher of our faith."
Hebrews 12:2

As human beings, we are often so eager to accomplish great tasks so soon. It most likely comes from societal pressure with people saying things like "By this age, you should have accomplished this that and the third." Or maybe, you see your friends "succeeding" in certain areas of their lives. People often allow that invisible pressure that society has in place to hover over them.

Hey! You're in a race! But this race is recorded and documented as the biography of your life. God is the Author and the Finisher. Let Him write and finish your story. When you feel impatient remember the most valued bestselling author has agreed to pen your life story. So—Look out! Your life is going to be awesome!

PRAYER

Precious Lord, teach me to be patient! Your timing is perfect. I understand that you cannot give me what I am not ready for. Mold me, shape me, and develop me so that when the time of my desires does come, I am ready to receive them. Help me not to define my success by looking at others. Thank you Lord! In Jesus' name. Amen.

Day 28 Worksheet/Notes

How were you able to apply this to your life today?

How were you able to see God in a new way?

Notes

DAY 29

"Open to me the gates of righteousness:
I will go into them, and I will praise the
LORD."
Psalm 118:19

The gates!!! Yes, the gates that bring us into true communion and worship with our Lord Jesus! You've read the book. Now that you have become familiar with the gates would you rather be inside or outside of them? I think we can all agree that inside the gates is where we want to be. Dwelling in the presence of God isn't optional for us. Yes, we have free will. But if you've gotten this far in the devotional—you want Jesus. You desperately desire to be in His presence.

Keep that fire! Stay tenacious in your pursuit of God! I'm rooting for you! God is rooting for you! I'm excited and believe your journey with God will be one to talk about!

PRAYER

Lord, I desperately desire your presence. I can never have too much of you! The deeper you take me, the deeper I desire to go. I'm in this for the long run! I love you Lord!
In Jesus' name. Amen.

Day 29 Worksheet/Notes

How were you able to apply this to your life today?

How were you able to see God in a new way?

Notes

DAY 30

"And Moses said unto God, 'Behold, when I come unto the children of Israel, and shall say unto them, The God of your fathers hath sent me unto you; and they shall say to me, What is his name? What Shall I say unto them?' And God said unto Moses, 'I AM THAT I AM': and he said, 'thus shalt thou say unto the children of Israel, I AM hath sent me unto you.'"
Exodus 3:13

I love this scripture. It's one of my favorites to quote! It forces individuals to depend on God for everything. After all, He says, "I AM." That means that He IS EVERYTHING. If He is "I AM," this means you put whatever it is that you need after that. For example:

I AM your healer.

I AM your provider.

I AM your Father.

I AM your best friend.

I AM your lawyer.

I AM your comfort.

I AM your doctor.

Whatever you need, He is that! Isn't it a blessing in itself to know that God IS everything we need?

PRAYER

Thank you Jesus, for being everything I need! I know I can come to you, and you will show up on my behalf in any area of my life! Give me boldness to call on you for everything I need. In Jesus' name. Amen.

Day 30 Worksheet/Notes

How were you able to apply this to your life today?

How were you able to see God in a new way?

Notes

DAY 31

"And, behold, I come quickly; and my reward is with me, to give every man according as his work shall be. I am Alpha and Omega, the beginning and the end, the first and the last."
Revelation 22:12, 13

We're human, we love appreciation and affection. It's great to know that Jesus is coming back for us with rewards. He says "I will give every man according as his work shall be."

Wow! That's powerful! When it comes to God our performances matter. Only what we do for Christ will last.

Let's take a little moment to reflect.

Am I performing well for God? Will I just make it to heaven or will I receive rewards when I get there?

Get all that God has for you! Don't settle for the mediocre. When God places a task in front of you, do it! Do it well! Do it with the right spirit. Most of ALL our Lord is coming quickly, let's position ourselves in the state of **worship** and stay ready!

PRAYER

Dear Lord, thank you for salvation! Thank you for the assurance that you're coming back for me. If there are any areas in my life that I may be settling in, not doing my best or overlooking, help me to identify them and put my best foot forward. Earthly rewards are nothing compared to what you have for me. I want my performance to be reward worthy!
Thank you Lord!
In Jesus' name. Amen.

Day 31 Worksheet/Notes

How were you able to apply this to your life today?

How were you able to see God in a new way?

Notes

Day 31 Worksheet/Notes

How has your relationship with God deepened since reading the first portion of this book?

How has your relationship with God progressed since DAY #1 of your devotions until now?

Consider sharing your testimony of what God has done for you to your friends, family, and even strangers! May God get the glory out of your life!

JOURNAL

JOURNAL

JOURNAL

JOURNAL

JOURNAL

JOURNAL

JOURNAL

JOURNAL

JOURNAL

JOURNAL

Notes

Chapter 1 The Misconception
1. Worship: (http://Oxforddictionaries.com)

Chapter 2 Lifestyle of Worship
1. Lifestyle: (http://Oxforddictionaries.com)

2. Temperate: (https://www.google.com/search?q=temperate)

Chapter 4 Growing in God
1. Secret: (https://www.google.com/search?q=definition+secret)

2. Dwell: (https://www.google.com/search?q=definition+dwell)

3. Develop: (https://www.google.com/search?q=develop)

Devotional: Day 11
1. Ease: (https://www.google.com/search?q=definition+of+ease)

Devotional: Day 21
2. Joy: (https://www.google.com/search?q=definition+of+joy)

3.Strength:(https://www.google.com/search?q=definition+of+str
ength)

Royalty Free Stock photos:
Pgs. 35, 47, 127: (https://www.Pixabay.com)
"Conversations with God" Album cover Photography: Bridgette Demir

Acknowledgments

God is so faithful! I must acknowledge Him first!

"Jesus you're *everything* to me! You've blessed my heart, spirit and soul! You've changed my life! Life with you never gets old!"

I also bless the Lord for Apostle Robert Davidson for speaking to me and comparing/likening me to the Prophetess Anna in the Bible. This is significant to me because I debated for a while about what the title of this book should be. I had many possible names but when Apostle Davidson spoke to me and compared me to Anna—how she stayed at the temple and stayed at the gates fasting, praying, and worshiping God, I was automatically drawn to the name "The Gates." Apostle Davidson and his wife Prophetess Patricia have both played a pivotal role in my life, for which I am extremely appreciative!

I'm thankful for those closest to me who believe in the call on my life and continuously cover me in prayer!

About The Author

Passion for Jesus with execution is how many would describe Shalayna Janelle! She carries a boldness, authority, surety, and sincere fear of the Lord. She loves Jesus and desires to see generations come to wholeness in Christ! Being fully committed to the call to win the lost and make disciples for Jesus Christ, her passion is to train and disciple individuals to know God, trust God, operate in their God-given authority and watch God move!

After high school at the age of 18, she moved to Los Angeles, Ca. where she actively serves in ministry—one of the many areas God has called her to. A light in Hollywood, she has been in commercials, film and television programs as well as having hosted on the Trinity Broadcasting Network (TBN) and JUCE TV (TBN's young adult Channel).

Shalayna is an international Preacher and Speaker. God has bestowed her with many gifts: preaching, singing/leading worship, and Christian mentorship to name a few. Along with this, the ministry "Foundation in Christ!" was birthed. It is a ministry that empowers and leads women to grow in God with Jesus Christ as their foundation.

"In life, my mandate is **Isaiah 61:1-3 & Luke 4:18, 19."**

As a worshipper, she crafts music with the intent to bring individuals closer to Jesus Christ with powerful lyrics and hope;

Leading others to worship God and walk with purpose!

She has been called to be a mouthpiece for Jesus in this generation! To reveal Jesus in Hollywood and across the globe! Jesus said...

"And I, if I be lifted up from the earth, will draw all men unto me" (John 12:32).

Sign up for My E-News Letter
At ShalaynaJanelle.com

Would you like to contact Shalayna Janelle?

Speaking Engagements
Contact@ShalaynaJanelle.com

Music & Worship Leading
Bookings@ShalaynaJanelle.com

Mentoring & Life Coaching
Coaching@ShalaynaJanelle.com

**Join Shalayna Live Monday Mornings on Periscope at
9am EST/ 6am PST
For her Monday Morning Manna-Festation Prayer
Broadcast.**

Other Resources by Shalayna Janelle

Thy Kingdom Come

Conversations with God-EP

(Available on Amazon, ITunes, Google Play, and other major online retailers!)